Carol Deacon's Little Book of
Easy Children's

Carol Deacon CAKES

www.caroldeaconcakes.com

Introduction

Cakes have been used to celebrate birthdays for centuries and throughout that time, enterprising bakers (and harassed parents) have tried to make their cake designs special and memorable. It is the ancient Greeks who are usually credited with being the first to place candles on them – some bright spark (pardon the pun) wanted to find a way to make their round cakes glow like the moon.

If you have never baked a cake or simply want to produce one fast, I hope this book will inspire you to have a go. You can make your cake as simple or as complicated as you like. I want you to enjoy these designs not to be intimidated by them. You don't need to have a cake covered with fairies or teddies, you could just make one or two and sit them stylishly on one edge of the cake.

Feel free to alter the size and shape of the cake too. I receive a lot of comments from people saying that they like my sponge recipe, but that in the book they've got it only goes up to a certain size and they want to bake a bigger cake. Again it's a case of not being frightened but having a go. Double or even triple the amounts quoted for a smaller sized cake and fill your tin! The worst case scenario is that you end up with either too much or too little mixture in which case you can bake a few fairy cakes with the leftover or make another small batch and gently stir in.

But sometimes, despite the best laid plans, time can still sneak up and defeat you. So to make you feel better, I'll let you into one of my most recent shameful secrets. Despite writing books about cake decorating I too have been known to leave it all a bit late and only a couple of months ago found myself producing a simple cake smothered with buttercream and sweets for one of my children, promising them something a bit more exotic at a later date when time allowed. But you know what, it didn't matter. For when the candles were lit and we were all singing "Happy Birthday" with gusto and a loud lack of melody I realised the real magic and power of a birthday cake. It's not just the technique, skill and time spent producing a masterpiece, it's in the light it brings to their eyes, the flush to their cheeks and the thrill of blowing out those candles. This is their special moment, their special day and the cake – no matter how lopsided or amazing - is positive sugary proof that someone loves them.

Happy Baking !

Contents

Introduction   2

Basic Equipment   4

Baking Your Cake   6

Buttercream   8

Sugarpaste   9

Colouring and Modelling Sugarpaste   10

Kitty on a Cushion   12

Racing Cars   14

Muddy Tractor   16

Teddy Bears   18

Toy Train   20

Sweet Dragon   22

Fairy Ring   24

Computer Game   26

(No) Treasure Island   28

Home Sweet Home   30

Cheeky Car   32

Magical Unicorn   34

Templates and Piping Bag   36

And Finally...   37

Basic Equipment

**Not everything here is essential and much of it you may have around your kitchen already.
Build your collection up gradually.**

1 Mixing Bowl
A large bowl is essential for mixing cake mixture and icing.

2 Wooden Spoon
Used for stirring cake mixture. The handle can also be used as a modelling tool.

3 Small Bowls
Use for holding water and icing sugar when decorating.

4 Teaspoon
For stirring and spooning small amounts of ingredients.

5 Cutters
Available in metal and plastic, there is a huge range available. Collect them as you go along. No cutters are essential for any cakes in this book.

6 Rolling Pins
A large rolling pin is essential for rolling out marzipan and sugarpaste. A small one is useful for small quantities but a paintbrush handle will work just as well.

7 Small Non-Serrated Knife
A small sharp knife with a straight blade is vital for neat clean cutting.

8 Paintbrushes
You need a medium brush for sticking models and a fine one for painting details. Sable brushes are expensive but are best and will last for ages. They are soft enough not to dent the sugarpaste and have a fine pointed tip for delicate painting.

9 Pencil
For tracing and drawing templates

10 Drinking Straw
Use as tiny circle cutters for making eyes. Held at an angle and pressed into an icing face, you can also use them to make smiles or frowns.

11 Pastry Brush
Used for spreading apricot jam over the fruitcake and moistening marzipan with water. You can also use them dry as a brush to gently clean your cakes.

12 Cocktail Stick
Use these to add food paste colour to sugarpaste. They can also be rolled over sugarpaste to make frills.

13 Spatula
Use for getting cake mixture and icing out of bowls.

14 Carving Knife
Use for slicing and shaping cakes.

15 Palette Knife
Useful for spreading jam and buttercream and loosening rolled out sugarpaste stuck to your work surface. Also makes a safe knife for small children to use.

16 Cake Smoother
Helps achieve a professional smooth finish when covering cakes with sugarpaste.

17 Tea Strainer
Useful for sieving small quantities of icing sugar "snow" over small areas.

18 Sieve
Use to sift lumps out of flour and icing sugar. Push icing through it to make good hair !

19 String
Tied around the paper on the outside of a baking tin when cooking fruit cake.

20 Turntable
Not essential but it does make cake decorating easier.

21 Scissors
Used for cutting string, tape and around templates

22 Small Plastic Food Bags
For storing sugarpaste and marzipan to prevent them hardening.

23 Tape Measure
Use for measuring circumference of boards and cakes and measuring ribbon.

24 Sticky Tape
Use a little bit at the back of a cake to hold ribbon in place.

25 Baking Tin
Used for baking cakes.

Baking Your Cake

Many people think baking a cake is extremely complicated but it really isn't. In this sponge cake recipe you just throw everything into a bowl together, mix it and bake. The added bonus is that it tastes delicious, there are no nasty chemicals or preservatives and you can freeze the end result for up to three months.

Madeira Sponge Cake

Square Tin Round Tin	15cm (6in)	15cm (6in) 20cm (8in)	20cm (8in)
Self Raising Flour	170g (6oz)	230g (8oz)	290g (10oz)	350g (12oz)
Caster sugar	115g (4oz)	170g (6oz)	230g (8oz)	290g (10oz)
Butter (soft)	115g (4oz)	170g (6oz)	230g (8oz)	290g (10oz)
Eggs (medium)	2	3	4	5
Milk	15ml (1tbsp)	30ml (2tbsp)	30ml (2tbsp)	45ml (3tbsp)
Baking time (approx)	1hr	1 1/4hrs	1 3/4hrs	2hrs

1 Line the tin and preheat your oven to 150C/300F/gas mark 2.

2 Sift the flour into a mixing bowl and add the rest of the ingredients. If using a mixer, start on a slow speed to bind the ingredients together then increase and beat on a faster speed for one minute until the mixture is pale and smooth. If you are mixing by hand, make sure the butter is really soft and mix with the sugar, stirring until it looks creamy. Mix in the eggs and milk until smooth and sloppy then gently fold in the flour using a metal spoon.

3 Spoon it into the prepared tin and bake in the centre of the oven. To test whether it's ready, first listen to it! If there are still a lot of bubbling sounds then it's probably not. Give it a further ten minutes. If it's quiet and pulling away from the sides slightly then test by inserting a knife or skewer. If it comes out clean then the cake is done. Leave in the tin for five minutes then turn out onto a wire rack. Peel away the greaseproof and leave to cool.

TIP: Sometimes cakes do odd things while baking. For example, you may find that the top has risen and cracked or one section has scorched. This does not render your project a disaster as the crust will usually be cut off a cake before it is decorated.

Tip: To soften butter quickly, microwave it for a few seconds.

Lining your Tin

Grease the inside of the tin by rubbing a little butter around it using a bit of paper towel. Cut a sheet of greaseproof long enough to go right round the tin and stand inside the tin to line it. The grease inside the tin should hold it in place. Using the baking tin itself as a template, draw around it on another piece of greaseproof. Cut the circle or square out and place inside the tin.

Fairy Cakes and Pudding Bowls

The 3 egg mixture should make at least 12 fairy cakes. Spoon into cake cases and bake for about 30 minutes.

To make a perfect rounded cake for designs such as the Unicorn, use the 3 egg mixture and bake in a 1 litre heatproof pudding bowl.

Grease the bowl first and place a disc of greaseproof paper in the base. When cooked, slide a knife around the edges of the cake to loosen it and turn it out.

Taste and colour variations

It's easy to vary the flavour of the cake. You could add a tablespoon of cocoa or instant coffee or some orange or lemon zest to the mixture before baking. Alternatively a teaspoon of almond essence or 60g (2 oz) of desiccated coconut will add a hint of something exotic. For a more colourful cake, add a handful of coloured chocolate beans (slightly crushed), chocolate chips or sliced glace cherries and mix them in before baking. Alternatively, add a swirl of food colour or two for a multi-coloured effect.

Different sized cakes

If you need to bake a bigger cake, simply double or triple the amounts given here. For instance for a 30cm (12in) square cake I'd probably do triple the 5 egg recipe. (Make the batches up separately if you only have a small bowl and gently stir together.)The mixture should reach two thirds of the way up the tin before baking. If you have too much, use the excess to make a few fairy cakes.

Storing and freezing your cake

Once cooled your sponge cake should be decorated and eaten within four days. Store in a cake box or tin. A plain undecorated sponge can be wrapped in plastic wrap and frozen for up to 3 months.

Microwave cakes

As it only take four minutes to cook, a microwave cake has a distinct environmental advantage over a conventionally baked cake. It will have a slightly different texture and look dreadfully pale when cooked but once decorated, it'll disappear with exactly the same speed as an oven baked cake! The amounts given are for an 18cm (7in) round microwave cake pan or a 1 litre heatproof pudding bowl. Never try and use a metal cake tin in a microwave.

Microwave Vanilla Sponge

120g (4oz) butter
120g (4oz) caster sugar
2 large eggs
1 teasp vanilla essence
120g (4oz) Self Raising flour
1/2 teasp baking powder

1 Grease the pan and place a disc of greaseproof paper on the base.

2 Cream the butter and sugar together.

3 Beat in the eggs and vanilla.

4 Stir in the flour and baking powder.

5 Spoon into the prepared pan and cook on full power for 4 minutes. Leave to stand for ten minutes then slide a knife around the edge of the cake and turn out.

Microwave Chocolate Sponge

120g (4oz) butter
120g (4oz) caster sugar
2 large eggs
90g (3oz) Self-Raising flour
1 teasp baking powder
30g (1oz) cocoa powder

1 Follow steps 1-3 as for the vanilla sponge cake above except this time leave out the vanilla essence.

2 Sieve and stir in the cocoa, flour and baking powder.

3 Cook on full for four minutes. Leave to stand for ten then run a knife around the edge of the pan and turn out the cake.

Using up leftovers to make chocolate cake truffles

If you're carving a cake into an unusual shape or levelling the top of the cake, you might have bits of cake left over. You can use these to make little cake truffles. You can use any type of cake (vanilla, chocolate or fruit) and any type of chocolate (milk, plain or white).

You will need approximately 30g (1oz) of chocolate to every 30g (1oz) of cake broken into crumbs. You can use any combination of cake and chocolate (Madeira and white chocolate go together particularly well!) Simply melt the chocolate, stir in the cake crumbs and roll into little balls. Decorate with sweets, chocolate or sifted icing sugar.

Buttercream

I like to use buttercream to both fill and coat my cakes before covering them with sugarpaste. The buttercream acts as a glue to hold the sugarpaste to the cake. You could use jam instead if you prefer.

This will make 1 quantity of buttercream. If you have some leftover, it can be stored in the fridge for a week or frozen for up to a month.

250g (8oz) softened butter
500g (1lb) sifted icing sugar
1 teasp vanilla essence
1 tbsp hot water

Beat the butter until soft and fluffy then add the rest of the ingredients. Continue to beat until it becomes creamy. Cover or store in a plastic airtight container until required.

Flavour variations

Stir 100g (3 1/2oz) melted plain or white chocolate into the buttercream.
Alternatively mix 1 tbsp cocoa powder and 1-2tbsp hot water into a paste and add that instead. If it becomes too runny, add more icing sugar.
For coffee buttercream mix 1tbsp instant coffee into 1 tbsp hot water and beat into the buttercream, or you could add a dash of peppermint, almond or lemon flavouring instead of the vanilla essence.

To buttercream your cake

Sometimes after you have sliced a cake to fill it with buttercream, you find the layers don't seem to fit properly when you put it back together again.

Here's a neat little trick to stop this happening.

1 Slice a little off the top of the cake if it has risen too much in the oven and turn it upside down.

2 Make a vertical buttercream mark down the side of the cake before you slice it.

3 Slice the cake into the required number of layers

4 Spread buttercream over the top of the bottom layer. Then - and here's the trick- place the next layer on top, lining the buttercream marks up with each other.

5 Continue with any additional layers making sure the buttercream marks line up. Your layers should now fit back neatly together.

Covering your cake with buttercream

After you have filled the centre of the cake place the cake on the board and spread buttercream around the sides and top. Spread buttercream around the sides first. This will allow you to hold the top steady with your other hand without getting too sticky.

TIP: If it's a hot day causing the buttercream to dry out quickly or you are not going to cover the cake immediately, cover the buttercreamed cake with a layer of plastic wrap until you're ready.

Colouring Buttercream

It is easy to colour buttercream if you wish. Try to use paste colours rather than liquid to stop the buttercream becoming too runny. Should this happen, mix a little icing sugar back in. If you are trying to limit your use of food colours, you can also stir a blob of jam into your buttercream. This will both add a bit of colour as well as a fruity tang.

Freezing Buttercream

Buttercream freezes well so if you find you have made too much, freeze the excess and keep frozen for up to a month.

Sugarpaste

Sugarpaste, also known as ready-to-roll, or rolled fondant icing is extremely easy to use even for the complete beginner. It is very similar to using modelling clay, except, of course, it is edible.

Sugarpaste is a wonderful type of icing to use as it is so versatile. You can roll it, make models with it, stretch it, cut it, press patterns and shapes into it. Even very young children can have fun making simple shapes and decorations – if you can stop them eating it that is !

You can buy sugarpaste from supermarkets, cake decorating shops (look up your nearest in the phone book) or via mail order on the internet. I always use shop-bought sugarpaste but it is perfectly possible to make your own if you prefer.

Sugarpaste Recipe

Ingredients

500g (1lb 2oz) icing sugar (confectioners' sugar)
1 egg white or equivalent amount of dried egg white (meringue powder) reconstituted
30ml (2 tbsp) liquid glucose (available from cake decorating equipment shops, some supermarkets and chemists/ drug stores)

Method

1 Put the sugar in a large bowl and make a well in the centre.

2 Tip the egg white (or reconstituted egg white /meringue powder) and glucose into the centre and stir in.

3 Use your hand to finish binding the icing together. Knead until the icing feels silky smooth.

4 Double wrap the icing in two small plastic food bags to stop it drying out. It can be used straight away and does not need to be kept in a refrigerator. Use within a week.

Covering your Cake

When using sugarpaste to cover a cake, always roll it out on a surface dusted with icing sugar to prevent it sticking to your work surface. The sugarpaste when rolled should be about 5mm (1/2in) thick.

You can either lift and place the icing over the top of the cake as you would pastry using a rolling pin, or slide your hands, palms uppermost underneath the icing and lift it keeping your hands flat. If you can feel it sticking to your worksurface, slide a palette knife underneath to loosen it.

If it all goes horribly wrong, scrunch it all up and roll it out again.

Once you have placed it over your cake, smooth the top into place using the flat of your hand. Smoothing the top before the

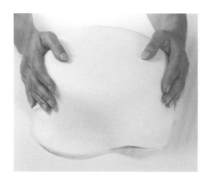

sides will help prevent air getting trapped and forming an unwanted air bubble. Then smooth the sides.

Trim away the excess from around the base with a small sharp unserrated knife.

Cake Smoothers

For a really professional finish, use a pair of cake smoothers. These are flat bits of plastic with a handle that you hold like an iron and use to run over the surface of the cake to literally iron out any lumps and bumps.

Air Bubbles

If an unsightly air bubble develops, prick it with a clean dressmaker's needle or cocktail stick held at an angle then carefully press out the air.

Storing

Cakes covered with sugarpaste should be stored in tins or cardboard cake boxes. They do not need to be stored in the fridge. Don't use airtight plastic containers or the icing will "sweat". Sugarpasted cakes are not suitable for freezing.

Colouring Sugarpaste

You can buy ready-coloured sugarpaste from cake decorating shops, some supermarkets and via the internet but it is easy to colour your own.

Try to use paste or gel colours (available from the same outlets as above) as these are thicker than liquid colourings and won't make your icing soggy if you are using quite a lot to achieve a deep colour.

Simply apply some dabs of food colour paste to the sugarpaste and knead it in. Try to avoid the urge to dip your modelling knife or paintbrush into the pot of colour and use a cocktail stick which you can throw away afterwards.

If you want to achieve a marbled effect, stop kneading before the icing turns one flat colour and the veins are clearly visible. You can knead more than one colour together at a time if you wanted to achieve a multi-coloured marbled effect.

For a solid block of colour there is no alternative but to continue kneading until the icing has turned a flat matt colour with no visible streaks.

You can also mix different colours of sugarpaste together such as a lump of red and yellow to make orange or white and black to make grey. To lighten a colour, knead in more white.

Flesh Tones

To make a pink flesh colour, either use a shade of food paste called "paprika" or knead a little pink, yellow and white sugarpaste together.

For darker tones, use a brown food colour paste or knead a little green, red and black sugarpaste together.

To make the golden brown colour for the teddy bears on page 18, use a shade of food colour paste called "Autumn Leaf". It is also possible to buy a ready coloured

sugarpaste called - rather aptly - Teddy Bear Brown which you can buy via a cake decorating shop or Internet.

Alternatively knead some red, yellow and a little black sugarpaste together or knead some yellow, red and a dash of black food colour paste into a blob of white sugarpaste.

Make up all your colours before you start your cake and store them in small plastic food bags until you are ready for them.

Painting on sugarpaste

It is perfectly possible to paint on sugarpaste using food colour paste and a fine paintbrush. Mix the colour with a little warer. It is a useful way to add a quirky mouth or details to your character or to put a message on a cake if you can't be bothered to make up a piping bag and pipe one.

If you go wrong, gently dab the mistake using a soft paintbrush and a little clean water to break the colour up.

Then wipe the mistake away with a clean cloth. Wait until the area dries before repainting.

Modelling with Sugarpaste

As well as covering cakes, sugarpaste is excellent for making models.

Making Models

I try to make up the colours that I need before I start my models as that's the bit I like least. Don't make all the components up and then try to stick them together, or the sugarpaste will start to dry out and crack. Make the individual pieces as you go along.

To use sugarpaste successfully, there are a few basic rules you need to follow.

1 Once the packet is opened, it will dry out when not in use so keep any unused icing tightly wrapped in small polythene food bags in a plastic container. It does not need to be kept in a fridge.
2 Always keep a bowl of icing sugar handy and use it for rolling the sugarpaste out on prior to covering a cake and also for stopping your fingers from becoming sticky.
3 Don't worry about getting dusty icing sugar marks on your models. Once you have finished your cake, brush them away with a soft damp paintbrush. The sugarpaste will look shiny for a while but it will eventually revert back to a matt finish.
4 Use a paintbrush to stick your models together with light dabs of cooled boiled water.
5 If your sugarpaste is very cold and hard (not to be confused with dried out and hard) you can soften it by microwaving it for about 10 seconds in the microwave. Do not over do it or it will melt.

Making Faces

There are all sorts of easy ways to make amusing faces on your characters with very little in the way of tools. Not only can a paintbrush be used for sticking models together, but its pointed end can also be

used for making an "O" shaped surprised mouth or the details on the end of a teddy bear's paw.

A drinking straw or piping nozzle held and pressed into your icing at an angle can be used to make both happy and sad mouths depending upon which way you hold it. The "U" shapes they make when pressed into sugarpaste also make wonderful scales on dragon or mermaid tails.

The tip of a cocktail stick dipped into a little black food colour makes neat same sized dots. Ideal for eyes on little models.

Candles

Although there's nothing wrong with a few candles in plastic holders stuck into the top of your cake, you can make your own holders that become part of the design.

Make sure the candle is safe before lighting. It must stand straight and securely and should be well away from anything that could catch fire.

For a pebble candle holder, partially knead a little grey and white sugarpaste together. Pull off little lumps and roll into pebble shapes.

For flowers and balls, use a simple flower shaped cutter to make thick flower shapes or roll lumps of sugarpaste into balls.

If using a character as a candle holder position the hands above the head. Securely press a candle into a plastic candle holder and insert into the top of your model character.

Colouring Desiccated Coconut

This has nothing to do with sugarpaste but is a very quick way to cover a board.

Green coloured coconut makes realistic "grass" and grey or brown coconut makes excellent "gravel". You can also colour granulated sugar in exactly the same way.

Place the coconut into a small bowl and add a small amount of food colour paste. Mix in the colour adding more as necessary. To prevent staining, you could wear a disposable plastic glove.

Kitty on a Cushion

The inspiration for this design came from two little girls called Amber and Anais who wanted a kitten cake. The result was so charming I thought other little girls (and boys) might like one too.

You will need

20cm (8in) square sponge cake
2 quantities buttercream (see page 8)
1 kg (2lb 4oz) white sugarpaste
350g (12oz) grey coloured sugarpaste
500g (1lb 2oz) pink coloured sugarpaste
1 strand raw, uncooked spaghetti
Black food colour paste
Small bowl icing sugar
Water for sticking

Equipment

30cm (12in) square cake board
Carving knife
Palette knife
Rolling pin
Cake smoothers (optional)
Small sharp knife
Paintbrush
Metal piping nozzle (any) or small lid
Ribbon

fig 1

TIP: You could make an icing ribbon if you prefer. Instructions are given in the Unicorn cake on page 34.

TIP: Leave the board plain if you feel the pink looks too difficult to do.

To decorate your cake

1 Round the corners and edges of the cake slightly then slice into two or three layers and reassemble, filling with buttercream. Place the cake in the centre of the board and coat the sides and top with buttercream.

2 Roll out and cover the cake using 1kg (2lb 4oz) white sugarpaste. Trim away and keep the excess from around the base.

3 Stick four small flattened white sugarpaste balls on top to make the buttons and press a few crease lines fanning out from them using the back of your knife.

4 For the kitten's body, roll 175g (6oz) grey sugarpaste into a flattish oval (fig 1) and stick on the cake. Roll 20g (2/3oz) grey sugarpaste into a sausage for his front paws. Cut it in half and stick next to the body. Press 3 lines into the tip of each paw with your knife.

5 Make a 90g (3oz) flattish grey ball shape for his head and stick on top of the body and paws. Press the edge of the piping nozzle into the icing at an angle to make the eyes and mouth.

6 Make two small grey triangles for ears and stick two smaller pink ones on top. Stick onto the head. Use 6 small pieces of spaghetti for the whiskers and a tiny pink ball for the nose.

7 For the back leg, make a 10g (1/3oz) grey oval for the paw and a 20g (2/3oz) thick disc shape for the thigh. Stick both in place and press claws as before.

fig 2

8 Roll 30g (1oz) grey sugarpaste into a tapering sausage shape for the tail. Stick it in place.

9 Make a 10g (1/3oz) grey oval for the mouse. Make a small flattish grey ball for the ears and stick a smaller pink one on top. Cut it in half and stick in place. Add a tiny pink nose and tail and two black food paste dots for eyes. Make a mouth with the piping nozzle. Stick behind the unsuspecting cat.

10 Moisten the exposed cake board with a little water. Knead and roll out the remaining pink sugarpaste. Cut it into strips and lay around the board scrunching it up to look a bit like fabric (fig 2). Neaten the edges.

11 To make the tassels, make four 10g (1/3oz) white ovals. Press lines down their lengths and slice a little off one end. Stick one at each corner. Make four 5g (1/8oz) white balls. Press lines into each one and stick one on each tassel.

12 Make a bow for the cat and hold it in place with a small blob of wet, sticky sugarpaste.

Racing Cars

These little cars look so sweet and would be perfectly suitable for grown up "boys" too. The quantities given are for ONE car so to get an idea of how much icing you will need, multiply the amounts by the number of cars you will be making.

You will need

As many cooked fairy cakes (cup cakes) as required (see page 6 for recipe)
Buttercream (1 quantity per 25 cakes)
Green food colour

For ONE car:

15g (1/2oz) sugarpaste for the car's body
5g (1/8oz) white sugarpaste
5g (1/8oz) sugarpaste for the driver's head
5g (1/8oz) black coloured sugarpaste
Black food colour paste
Small bowl icing sugar
Water for sticking

Equipment

Small sharp knife
Small rolling pin (optional – see tip below)
Fine paintbrush
Small round cutter, piping nozzle or lid (optional – see step 3)
Drinking straw
Cocktail stick (optional)

fig 1

To decorate your cake

1 Begin by making the body of the car. Decide what colour the body of your car should be and roll 10g (1/3oz) of that colour sugarpaste into a short carrot shape about 4cm (1 1/2in) long (fig 1).

2 Thinly roll out a little of the same colour sugarpaste to a thickness of about 2mm (1/8 in) and cut out a tiny rectangle about 2cm X 8mm (3/4in X 1/4in). Stick on the back of the car.

3 Thinly roll out about 5g (1/8oz) white sugarpaste (see the tip below for rolling out small quantities). Using something small and circular like a piping nozzle, cut out a thin flat white disc and stick towards the pointed end of the car's body with a dab of water. If you have no cutter, make a tiny white sugarpaste ball and squash it !

4 Make a small pea-sized ball for the driver's head and stick on top of the car. Make a tiny flesh coloured sugarpaste ball and flatten it into an oval shape. Stick it on the front of the driver's head.

5 For the wheels, roll 5g (1/8oz) black sugarpaste into an oval about 2.5cm (1in) long and slice it into four equal discs.

6 Stick the wheels in place around the car. Carefully press the end of a drinking straw once into each wheel to add a bit of detail (fig 2). Repeat the whole process making as many cars as you need.

7 Paint your numbers on the cars with a fine paintbrush and a little black food colour. Make two dots for eyes on each driver's face using your paintbrush or a cocktail stick.

8 When all your cars are ready, colour a little buttercream green. Spread about a teaspoonful on top of a cake and a place car on top.

fig 2

TIP: You may find it quicker and easier to make five or six of the same colour car at the same time.

TIP: You can use your paintbrush as a mini rolling pin to flatten the white icing circles.

Muddy Tractor

As well as being very tasty, chocolate buttercream makes excellent "mud". Use blobs to cover any problem areas on your tractor. Other items from around the kitchen can be used to make special effects too. Dark brown sugar can look like moist earthy soil, while light brown sugar makes brilliant "sand".

You will need

15cm (6in) square sponge cake
2 quantities chocolate buttercream (see page 8)
1kg (2lb 4oz) blue coloured sugarpaste
700g (1lb 9oz) black coloured sugarpaste
30g (1oz) white sugarpaste
150g (5oz) pink coloured sugarpaste
Black food colour paste
1 liquorice sweet (optional)
Small bowl icing sugar
Water for sticking

Equipment

25cm (10in) round cake board
Carving knife
Palette knife
Rolling pin
Cake smoothers (optional)
Small sharp knife
Paintbrush
3 small lids or circle cutters – about 4cm, 3cm & 2cm (1 1/2in, 1in & 3/4in) diameters.
Mudguard template (see page 36)

fig 1

TIP: An alternative way to make a large wheel shape is to cover a large biscuit with 100g (3 1/2oz) black sugarpaste. Use water to stick it to the biscuit. See car cake on page 32.

To decorate your cake

1 To get the basic tractor shape, follow the first three steps for making the car cake on page 32. Cover the cake using 800g (1lb 12oz) blue sugarpaste instead of green.

2 For the large wheels, make two 200g (7oz) black sugarpaste balls. Squash each one into a thick disc about 9cm (3 1/2in) in diameter. Stick them in place against the sides of the tractor.

3 Make two smaller wheels using 90g (3oz) black sugarpaste per wheel and stick towards the front of the tractor. Press a few lines into the edges of each wheel using the back of your knife (fig 1)

4 Dab a little water on the roof of the tractor. Roll out about 90g (3oz) black sugarpaste and cut out a rectangle about 11cm X 8cm (4 1/2in X 3in). Stick it on top of the tractor.

5 Thinly roll out about 45g (1 1/2oz) blue sugarpaste and using the largest circle cutter or small lid, cut out 2 discs. Press a smaller circle into each disc (don't go right through) and stick one on each big wheel. Make two smaller discs for the smaller wheels.

6 To make the rear wheel mudguards, thinly roll out about 45g (1 1/2oz) blue sugarpaste. Cut out two rounded rectangular shapes using the template if necessary. Stick them on top of the largest wheels.

7 Make two 5g (1/8oz) white balls for they eyes and stick in place. Decorate with two small flattened black icing balls and two tiny white ones.

8 Roll 10g (1/3oz) blue sugarpaste into a ball for the headlights. Cut it in half and stick on the front of the tractor's bonnet. Cut out two flat white discs and stick one on the front of each headlight. Press the back of your knife into each one to make a criss-cross pattern.

9 To make a pig, first make a 30g (1oz) pink ball for its body (fig 2). Make a 5g (1/8oz) pink ball for its snout. Flatten the snout slightly and stick on the larger ball. Poke the end of your paintbrush into the snout twice to make nostrils.

fig 2

10 Thinly roll out about 10g (1/3oz) pink sugarpaste and cut out two small squares for the ears. Stick on the side of the head. Make another two pigs.

11 To finish, paint two black food colour lines for the tractor's eyebrows and a wavy line for his mouth. Paint two dots on each pig for eyes. Stick a liquorice sweet on the bonnet to make the funnel and spread chocolate buttercream "mud" over the board. Position the pigs and smear a little "mud" over them.

TIP: If when you're covering the cake, your icing bunches up into folds at the back , hide them with buttercream "mud".

Teddy Bears

At first glance you might think this is a difficult project, but in fact teddy bears are really easy to do. Although there are thirteen of them, you could spread things out and make them over a few nights prior to decorating the cake.

You will need

20cm (8in) round sponge cake
1 quantity buttercream (see page 8)
1 kg (2lb 4oz) white sugarpaste
800g (2lb) golden brown coloured sugarpaste (see page 10)
Black food colour paste
Small bowl of icing sugar
Water for sticking

Equipment

25cm (10in) round cake board
Carving knife
Palette knife
Rolling pin
Cake smoother (optional)
Small sharp knife
Paintbrush
Small circle cutter or lid (see "TIP" below)
Cocktail stick

fig 1

TIP: If you do not have a circle cutter or suitable lid for making his tummy, make a small white icing ball, flatten it, and use that instead.

To decorate your cake

1 Level the top of your cake if necessary and turn upside-down. Slice the cake into two or three layers and reassemble sandwiching the layers together with buttercream.

2 Place the cake in the centre of the cake board and spread a thin coating of buttercream around the sides and top. Knead the white sugarpaste until pliable. Roll it out and lift and cover the cake.

3 Smooth the icing over the cake and cut away any excess from around the base. Keep the leftover white for making the bears' muzzles and tummies later.

4 To make a bear, begin with his body. Roll about 20g (2/3oz) brown sugarpaste into an oval and stand upright (fig 1). Dab a little water on the top. Make a 10g (1/3oz) ball for his head and stick on top of the body.

5 Stick a small white sugarpaste oval on the lower part of the head to form his muzzle.

6 Thinly roll out about 10g (1/3oz) white sugarpaste and using a small circle cutter or lid, cut out a circle and stick it onto the bear's tummy. (See "TIP")

7 For the legs, roll about 10g (1/3oz) icing into a sausage about 6cm (2 1/2in) long. Cut it in half and squash and bend the end of each leg to make two "L" shapes. Stick one either side of the bear's body and press four small hollows into each foot using the end of your paintbrush.

8 Make two small brown sausage shapes for arms and stick in place. Make two tiny balls for ears and stick onto the head.

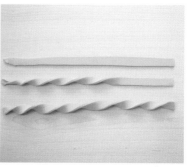

fig 2

Press a small hollow into each one with the end of your paintbrush.

9 Dip the tip of a cocktail stick into a little black food colour and make two dots for eyes and one for a nose. You could also make a dot for a mouth or paint a smile with your paintbrush.

10 Make a further 12 bears and stick around the edge of the cake.

11 Paint a light line of water around the exposed cake board around the base of the cake.

12 Roll about 200g (7oz) brown sugarpaste into a long sausage. Flatten it by rolling over it with a rolling pin and cut out a strip about 60cm X 1.5cm (24in X 1/2 in). Slide a knife along under the strip to make sure it's not stuck to your work surface.

13 Carefully twist the sugarpaste then lift and starting from the back, lay it around the cake. Cut off any excess and stick the two ends together with a dab of water.

TIP: The twist around the base is a simple way to finish a cake but you could use ribbon or pipe or stick sweets around the base instead.

Toy Train

You could simplify this design by covering the cake with green coloured buttercream instead of green sugarpaste. If you do this, rough the buttercream up a little with a fork to look like grass.

You will need

20cm (8in) round sponge cake
1 quantity buttercream (see page 8)
1 kg (2lb 4oz) green coloured sugarpaste
120g (4oz) red coloured sugarpaste
120g (4oz) black coloured sugarpaste
20g (2/3oz) white sugarpaste
60g (2oz) yellow coloured sugarpaste
60g (2oz) blue coloured sugarpaste
Black food colour paste
Small bowl of icing sugar
Water for sticking

Equipment

25cm (10in) round cake board
Carving knife
Palette knife
Rolling pin
Small sharp knife
Paintbrush
Drinking straw
Piping nozzle or small lid
Cocktail stick
Sieve or garlic press (washed!)

fig 1

TIP: If you have a lot of leftover buttercream or you don't have a sieve, use dabs of green buttercream to make bushes. Fluff it up with your paintbrush.

To decorate your cake

1 Carve a few chunks out of the top of the cake. Split and fill the cake with buttercream. Place the cake on the board. Spread buttercream around the outside.

2 Knead and roll out the green sugarpaste. Cover the cake and trim and neaten around the base. Keep the leftover icing.

3 Use the back of you knife to press two lines about 2.5cm (1in) apart around the top edge of the cake for the track. Then press lines about 1cm (1/4in) apart across the track to make the sleepers.

4 For the engine's cab, roll 30g (1oz) red sugarpaste into an upright oval about 3.5cm (1 1/2in) high (fig 1). Make a second 15g (1/2oz) red oval about 2.5cm (1in) long and stick at a right angle to the first. Poke a small hole with the end of a paintbrush in the front of the engine to make a mouth.

5 Roll out 10g (1/3oz) black sugarpaste to a 5mm (1/4in) thickness and cut out a 3cm (1 1/4in) square. Stick it on top of the cab. Make two 5g (1/8oz) black discs for the rear wheels. Stick one either side of the engine's cab.

6 Make another four smaller wheels and stick two either side of the engine. Add a bit of detail to each wheel by pressing a circle into the centre of each wheel with the tip of a drinking straw.

7 Make two tiny white balls for eyes and stick in place. Make a small black icing oval for a funnel and stick towards the front of the engine. Make two small black leaf shapes for the moustache and stick in place. Add a tiny red icing ball for his nose.

fig 2

8 To make a carriage, roll 30g (1oz) yellow icing into an oval (fig 1). Press a mouth into the front of the carriage using a piping nozzle held at an angle. Make eyes and nose as before.

9 Press two eyebrows over the eyes using the piping nozzle and press a couple of hollows down the length of the carriage using the end of your paintbrush. Make 6 black wheels and stick down the length of the carriage.

10 Make another 6 different coloured carriages, altering the expressions if you wish. Press a piping nozzle upright and you make your carriage smile. Press it in the other way and he'll frown!

11 Dip a cocktail stick in black food colour and press a dot on each eyeball. Arrange and stick the train around the the cake.

12 To make the bushes, paint a light circle of water in the centre of the cake. Take a small lump of green sugarpaste and press it through the sieve or garlic press (fig 2). Slice off the sugarpaste strands and stick on the water. Continue until you have a circle of green bushes. Make more bushes and stick around the base of the cake.

Sweet Dragon

Putting sweets on a child's cake is ALWAYS a guarantee of success and by surrounding your character with them and hiding much of its body, you cut down on the amount of modelling you have to do.

You will need

20cm (8in) round sponge cake
2 quantities buttercream (see page 8)
150g (5oz) green coloured sugarpaste
10g (1/3 oz) white sugarpaste
5g (1/8oz) yellow coloured sugarpaste
Black food colour
Assorted small sweets
Small bowl of icing sugar
Water for sticking

Equipment

25cm (10in) round cake board
Carving knife
Palette knife
Small sharp knife
Paintbrush
Drinking straw
Dragon eye template (see page 36)

fig 1

TIP: You can make your dragon well ahead of time if you wish to save time on cake decorating day.

To decorate your cake

1 Begin with by making the dragon. Make a 20g (2/3oz) green sugarpaste ball for the dragon's neck (fig 1). Squash it slightly. Make a 75g (2 1/2oz) tapering green sausage shape for his head. Stick it onto the neck with a dab of water allowing the thinnest end to rest on your work surface.

2 Press a line for his mouth using the edge of your knife. Poke the end of a paintbrush into the end of his nose to make two nostrils. Holding a drinking straw at a slight angle, press some "U" shaped scales over the dragon's head. (fig 2)

3 Flatten a tiny bit of white icing and cut out two leaf shapes for the dragon's eyes. Stick them in place. Make two tiny green sausage shapes for his eyebrows and bend into "S" shapes. Stick one over each eye.

4 Make two tiny green triangles for ears. Make an indent in both using the end of your paintbrush and stick on the head. Make a further three triangles and stick down the back of his head and neck.

5 Make two 5g (1/8oz) green sausage shapes for his arms and stick next to the head. Flatten the paws slightly and make scales as before. Make 8 tiny yellow carrot shapes for the claws and teeth and stick on the hands and mouth.

6 Make a 5g (1/8oz) green carrot shape for his tail. Top with another small green icing triangle. Paint a black food colour dot on each eye and place the two dragon sections to one side.

fig 2

7 Level the top of your cake if necessary and turn upside-down. Slice the cake into two or three layers and reassemble sandwiching the layers together with buttercream.

8 Place the cake in the centre of the cake board and spread a liberal coating of buttercream around the sides and top.

9 Place the two dragon sections in place on the cake and arrange small sweets around the top and base of cake to finish.

TIP: You could alter this design by substituting a figure or animal instead of a dragon. Or for a really quick cake – just cover with sweets !

Fairy Ring

"Don't step in a fairy ring or you will be taken to the fairylands and trapped there forever" goes the saying. But as I don't suppose you're likely to put this cake on the floor and stand on it, I think you're pretty safe with this design!

You will need

20cm (8in) round sponge cake
1 quantity buttercream (see page 8)
1 kg (2lb 4oz) white sugarpaste
90g (3oz) red sugarpaste
180g (6oz) flesh coloured sugarpaste
60g (2oz) pink sugarpaste
180g (6oz) green sugarpaste
Black food colour paste
2 sheets edible wafer paper (rice paper)
Small bowl of icing sugar
Water for sticking

Equipment

25cm (10in) round cake board
Carving knife
Palette knife
Rolling pin
Cake smoother (optional)
Small sharp knife
Paintbrush
Cocktail stick
Piping bag (see TIP below and page 36)
Wing and leaf templates (see page 36)
Scissors

fig 1

TIP: To reduce the amount of modelling, just make the fairies on top of the cake and tie a ribbon around the base.

To decorate your cake

1 Level the top of your cake if necessary and turn it upside-down. Slice the cake into two or three layers and reassemble sandwiching the layers together with buttercream.

2 Place the cake in the centre of the cake board and spread a thin coating of buttercream around the sides and top. Keep the leftover buttercream for the hair later. Knead the white sugarpaste until pliable. Roll it out and lift and cover cake.

3 Smooth the icing over the cake and cut away and keep any excess from around the base.

4 To make a toadstool, first roll about 15g (1/2oz) white sugarpaste into an oval and stand it upright (fig 1). Dab a little water on top.

5 Roll 5g (1/8oz) red sugarpaste into a ball and flatten slightly. Stick this on top of the white. Make another 5 toadstools and stick around the top of the cake.

6 Make a further 6 toadstools and stick around the base of the cake. Make sure the red tops do not over hang the edges of the cake board. Then stick 3 flattened white balls on the top of each toadstool.

7 To make a fairy, start with the legs. First roll 5g (1/8oz) flesh coloured sugarpaste into a thin string (fig 2). Bend it in half and stick between two of the toadstools.

8 Shape 5g (1/8oz) pink sugarpaste into a triangle and stick on top of the legs. Make a small flesh coloured ball for the head and two thin strings for the arms. Stick them all in position. Make a further 5 fairies for the top of the cake and 6 for the base.

fig 2

9 Dip the tip of a cocktail stick into a black food colour and use it to make two small dots on each fairy's face.

10 Place about a tablespoon of buttercream in your piping bag, fold the end over to close it and snip a tiny triangle off the end. Pipe a good head of swirly hair on each fairy.

11 Cut a small heart shape out of rice paper and press one set of wings into the hair. Repeat on all the fairies.

12 To make a leaf, thinly roll out the green sugarpaste and cut out a leaf shape using the template if necessary. Press a few veins into it with the back of your knife and stick onto the cake between a fairy and a toadstool. Repeat making a further 23 leaves.

TIP: If you don't have a piping bag, you can snip a tiny corner off a plastic food bag and use that instead. Alternatively you could use a tube of "writing icing" from the supermarket or simply dab a little buttercream on each fairy using the tip of your knife.

Computer Game

Hand held game consoles appeal to all ages. The chap on this cake is wearing jeans so it would be easy to adapt him into a girl by changing the hairstyle and perhaps giving her a few painted on eyelashes.

You will need

20cm (8in) round sponge cake
1 quantity buttercream (see page 8)
1kg (2lb 4oz) white sugarpaste
60g (2oz) blue coloured sugarpaste
30g (1oz) flesh coloured sugarpaste
5g (1/8oz) yellow coloured sugarpaste
15g (1/2oz) black coloured sugarpaste
1 strand raw, uncooked spaghetti
Black food colour paste
Assorted tubes of "Writing icing" (see TIP below)
Small bowl icing of sugar
Water for sticking

Equipment

25cm (10in) round cake board
Carving knife
Palette knife
Rolling pin
Cake smoothers (optional)
Small sharp knife
Paintbrush
Piping nozzle or small lid
70cm (27in) ribbon
Sticky tape to secure ribbon

fig 1

To decorate your cake

1   Level the top of your cake if necessary and turn upside-down. Slice the cake into two or three layers and reassemble sandwiching the layers together with buttercream.

2   Place the cake in the centre of the cake board and spread a thin coating of buttercream around the sides and top. Knead the white sugarpaste until pliable. Roll it out and lift and cover cake.

3   Smooth the icing over the cake and cut away the excess from around the base. Pick out any crumbs and cover and put to one side.

4   To make the boy, roll 60g (2oz) blue sugarpaste into a sausage about 20cm (8in) long (fig 1). Cut off the two rounded ends. Bend the icing into a "U" shape and stick on top of the cake.

5   Make a 30g (1oz) white oval shape for the body and stick on top of the legs. Poke a little spaghetti through the body into the cake to provide extra support. Leave about 1.5cm (1/2in) protruding.

6   For the arms roll 15g (1/2oz) white sugarpaste into a sausage about 10cm (4in) long. Cut the sausage in half and stick one either side of the body. Use the rounded ends to make the shoulders.

7   Roll 20g (2/3oz) flesh coloured sugarpaste into a ball for his head and stick on top of the body. Add two tiny flattened white balls for eyes.

8   Make two tiny flesh coloured balls for ears and a third for a nose. Poke the end of a paintbrush into each ear to add a bit of detail. Paint two black food colour dots on the eyes

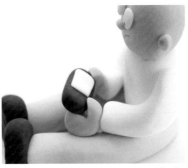

fig 2

9   Holding a piping nozzle at a slight angle, press a down-turned mouth into the lower part of his face. Make a tiny yellow rectangle for his hair. Press a few lines into it with the back of your knife and lay and stick over his head.

10   Make a small black oval shape for the games console and stick a tiny flat white icing rectangle on the front. Place to one side.

11   Make two small flesh coloured balls for hands and flatten them slightly. Make a partial cut into both hands to form thumbs and stick one on the end of each arm. Carefully put the console in place with the thumbs on top (fig 2).

12   Make two 5g (1/8oz) black oval shapes for his feet and stick in place.

13   To finish, pipe a few swirls or dots around the top of the cake and stand ribbon around the base. Secure it at the back with a little sticky tape.

TIP: You can buy ready coloured tubes of "writing icing" from the supermarket. Alternatively you could pipe coloured buttercream, paint some food colour squiggles or simply stick a few sweets around the cake instead.

(No) Treasure Island

Poor pirate, thanks to the sneaky octopus, he'll never find his treasure no matter how hard he looks. As you will be cutting chunks out of this cake to make it into an irregular island shape, it doesn't really matter what your cake does whilst it's baking in the oven – the more misshapen the better! If you don't have any chocolate coins use sweets instead.

You will need

20cm (8in) round sponge cake
2 quantities buttercream (see page 8)
750g (1lb 8oz) yellow coloured sugarpaste
100g (3 1/2oz) white sugarpaste
200 (7oz) green coloured sugarpaste
15g (1/2oz) black coloured sugarpaste
10g (1/3oz) brown coloured sugarpaste
Black & blue food colour pastes
4 rectangular biscuits (1 cut in half)
8 chocolate coins
Small bowl icing sugar
Water for sticking

Equipment

25cm (10in) round cake board
Carving knife
Palette knife
Rolling pin
Small sharp knife
Cake smoothers (optional)
Paintbrush
Small circle cutter, piping nozzle or lid

fig 1

TIP: Use a paintbrush to ease the buttercream into awkward areas around the tentacles and coins.

To decorate your cake

1   Cut a few dips and hollows out of the sides and top of the cake. Then slice the cake in half and fill with buttercream. Reassemble the cake and place it on the cake board. Spread a thin coating of buttercream over the sides and top.

2   Dust your work surface with icing sugar and knead the yellow sugarpaste until pliable. Roll it out to a thickness of about 5mm (1/4in) and place it over the cake. Gently smooth it into place and trim around the base. Keep any excess.

3   To make the treasure chest, stand two whole biscuits and the two half biscuits upright in a rectangle on top of the cake (fig 1). Press them gently into the icing. Make a 75g (2 1/2oz) white oval for the pirate's body and place inside the chest. It should both fill it and stand higher than the top of the chest.

4   Roll 60g (2oz) green sugarpaste into a sausage about 19cm (7 1/2in) long for the legs. Bend into a "U" shape and stick it in place.

5   Roll 10g (1/3oz) black sugarpaste into a small sausage for his boot. Bend it into an "L" shape and stick on the end of one leg. To make his wooden leg, stick a small brown oval and carrot shape on the end of the other leg.

6   Paint some stripes on his top with a fine paintbrush and some black food colour. Place the last biscuit in place to form the lid of the chest. Use a little blob of sticky sugarpaste to keep it in place.

fig 2

7   Make a 30g (1oz) green sugarpaste ball for the head of the octopus (fig 2) and stick it in place. Holding a small circle cutter or similar at an angle, poke it into the lower part of his head to make a smile.

8   Make five 20g (2/3oz) long green sausage shapes for tentacles. Stick them in place with the ends bent around the chocolate coins as if holding them. Add two small white sugarpaste balls for his eyes. Paint a black dot on each eye.

9   Partially stir a little blue food colour into the remaining buttercream. Swirl it around the cake board to make a fierce tempestuous sea!

10   To make the rocks, partially knead the rest of the black into the rest of the white to get a marbled effect. Break off and stick small irregular shaped lumps around the cake and sea.

TIP: The rocks on top of the cake can also double up as ideal birthday cake candle holders. Simply stand the candles securely in them well away from the pirate.

Home Sweet Home

As well as tasting great, a slice of Battenberg cake makes a fantastic ready-made window. If you cannot get hold of it or simply do not like it, use small squares of sugarpaste or squared sweets or biscuits instead.

You will need

20cm (8in) square sponge cake
2 quantities buttercream (see page 8)
2 packs rectangular shortcake biscuits (or similar)
2 chocolate finger biscuits
2 packs mini marshmallows
6 slices Battenberg cake (about 1cm (1/4in) thick)
1 pack liquorice sweets (optional – substitute other sweets if you prefer)
1 edible gold or silver ball (optional – you can use a round sweet instead)
Green food colour paste

Equipment

25cm (10in) round cake board
Carving knife
Palette knife
Plastic wrap
Small bowl
Fork

fig 1

TIP: If you can't get hold of white marshmallows use small cubes of white sugarpaste instead.

To decorate your cake

1 Cut across the middle of the cake to make two rectangles. Slice one half into two or three layers. Sandwich the layers together with buttercream and stand on the cake board. Spread a thick layer of buttercream over the top.

2 Carefully cut the second rectangle of cake into a long triangular shape for the roof and stand on top of the first section of cake on the board. You should now have a basic house shape (fig 1).

3 Spread a thick, soft coating of buttercream over the sides and top.

4 To make the door, press an upright biscuit into the front of the house. Stand a chocolate finger biscuit either side of the door.

5 Stick a line of mini marshmallows around the base of the house excluding the door.

6 Press the Battenberg windows into place removing the marzipan if you wish. Stick two at the front and back and one on either side (fig 2).

7 Press marshmallows into the exposed buttercream around the house to look like brickwork.

8 To tile the roof, lay a line of biscuits along the base of the roof on both sides. Lay a second line (and possibly a third depending on the size of your biscuits) on top until the roof is covered. Use dabs of buttercream to hold them in place.

fig 2

9 Place a square sweet or sugarpaste square on the centre of the ridge of the roof to make a chimney.

10 Press a line of marshmallows along the ridge of the roof either side of the chimney to neaten it.

11 Stick an edible silver ball or round sweet on the front door with a dab of buttercream to make the door handle.

12 Colour the remaining buttercream green and spread it around the exposed cake board.

13 "Fluff" the green icing up a bit with a fork to make it look like grass and press a few sweets into the grass to finish.

TIP: You could also decorate your house with a few fairies or teddies (see pages 18 & 24).

TIP: Place a strip of plastic wrap over the roof area to stop the buttercream drying out while you decorate the sides.

Cheeky Car

If you don't have a 15cm (6in) baking tin, either bake a larger cake and use a bigger board or trim a larger cake to fit. You will need to leave about 5cm (2in) either side of the shaped cake so that the wheels will fit onto the board. These wheels are made using biscuits. For solid icing wheels, follow instructions for the Tractor cake on page 16.

You will need

15cm (6in) square sponge cake
1 quantity buttercream (see page 8)
1 kg (2lb 4oz) green coloured sugarpaste
800g (1lb 10oz) black coloured sugarpaste
45g (1 1/2oz) grey coloured sugarpaste
120g (4oz) white sugarpaste
15g (1/2oz) yellow coloured sugarpaste
4 large biscuits
30g (1oz) desiccated coconut
Black food colour paste
Small bowl icing sugar
Water for sticking

Equipment

25cm (10in) round cake board
Carving knife
Palette knife
Rolling pin
Cake smoothers (optional)
Small sharp knife
Paintbrush
4cm (1 1/2in) & 3cm (1in) round circle cutters or small lids
Mudguard template (page 36)

fig 1

TIP: Use green or chocolate buttercream to make "mud" or "grass" around your car if you don't like coconut.

To decorate your cake

1 Cut about a 4cm (1 1/2in) strip off one side of the cake. Place the smaller section on top of the remaining cake.

2 Place the cake on the cake board. "Glue" the smaller section in place with buttercream. If you wish you can slice the cake into layers and fill them with buttercream too (fig 1). Spread buttercream over the top and sides.

3 Knead 800g (1lb 12oz) green sugarpaste until pliable. Roll it out to about 5mm (1/4in) thick. Place over the cake and smooth into place. (It may gather in folds at the back) Trim base and keep excess.

4 Paint a light line of water around the base of your car. Roll out 120g (4oz) black sugarpaste. Cut a thin strip 56cm X 2.5cm (22in X 1in). Roll the strip up like a bandage and starting from the back of the car, unwind and stick around base (fig 2).

5 For the wheels, paint a little water over a chocolate biscuit. Roll out about 100g (3 1/2oz) black sugarpaste and wrap around the biscuit. Stick in position and press a few tread lines around the edge of the wheel with the back of your knife. (See Tractor cake page 16) Make four wheels.

6 Thinly roll out the grey sugarpaste and using the larger circle cutter or lid, cut out 4 discs. Press the smaller circle cutter into each disc (don't go right through) to leave a round impression in the middle and stick one on each wheel.

7 Roll out 30g (1oz) green sugarpaste and cut out a mudguard. Use the template if necessary. Stick it on top of a wheel. Make another three and stick in place.

fig 2

8 Thinly roll out about 10g (1/3oz) white icing and cut out a small rectangle for a number plate. Stick on the front of the car.

9 Make two 30g (1oz) white icing balls and stick on top of the car for his eyes. Stick two flat black sugarpaste discs on the eyes. Add two flattened white balls for highlights.

10 For the headlights, make a 60g (2oz) green sugarpaste ball and cut in half. Stick on the front of the car. Make two flat yellow sugarpaste discs and stick one on each headlight. Press a few criss-cross lines across each yellow light with the back of your knife.

11 Using a fine paintbrush and black colour paint eyebrows, mouth and a message or number on the number plate.

12 Mix a little black food colour into the coconut to turn it grey and sprinkle over the board. (See page 11 for details)

TIP: If you don't want to paint a mouth, press the edge of a cutter into the icing to make a smile.

Magical Unicorn

Lose the horn and this design becomes a pony cake instead. You could pipe a buttercream mane and tail if you prefer. Remember to cover the board before the cake.

You will need

15cm (6in) round cake or pudding bowl cake (see page 6)
1 quantity buttercream (see page 8)
250g (8oz) green coloured sugarpaste
1.5 kg (3lb 6oz) white sugarpaste
150g (5oz) pink coloured sugarpaste
60g (2oz) yellow coloured sugarpaste
1 ice cream cone
Black food colour paste
Small bowl of icing sugar
Water for sticking

Equipment

25cm (10in) round cake board
Rolling pin
Small sharp knife
Carving knife
Palette knife
Cake smoothers (optional)
Fish slice (spatula)
Paintbrush

fig 1

To decorate your cake

1 Begin by covering the board. Moisten it with a little water. Partially roll out the green sugarpaste then place it on the board and continue to roll it up to and over the edges. Trim and neaten the edges and place the board to one side.

2 If you are using a round cake, carve a little off the top edge to make it rounded. If you baked your cake in a bowl, check the base is flat. Slice a little off if necessary.

3 Split the cake into three layers and fill with buttercream. Reassemble spreading a thin coating of buttercream over the sides.

4 Knead and roll out about 800g (1lb 12oz) white sugarpaste and place over the cake (fig 1). Smooth it into place and trim and neaten around the base.

5 Carefully lift the covered cake (you may find a fish slice or spatula useful). Place it towards the rear of the covered board.

6 Roll 200g (7oz) white icing into a slightly tapering oval shape for the head and stick it in place with a little water. The chin should rest on the board. Poke two nostrils in the end of the nose using the end of your paintbrush.

7 Make two 45g (1 1/2oz) white carrot shapes for the front legs and stick in place. Make two 120g (4oz) sausage shapes for the rear legs. Squash one end of each leg to make a thigh and flatten the other to form a hoof. Bend in half and stick in place with the hoof at the rear of the horse.

8 Carefully slice the bulbous end off an ice cream cone and press it into the top of the head. Use a little buttercream as "glue".

9 Make two 15g (1/2oz) white triangles for the ears and stick two smaller pink ones on top. Stick an ear either side of the horn.

10 Paint the eyes and mouth using a black food colour and a fine brush.

11 Knead a little yellow icing into 200g (4oz) white to make cream. Cut out 7 or 8 short strips and 4 or 5 strips 10cm (4in) long for the mane. Stick them in place adding more if you wish.

12 Make a 45g (1 1/2oz) cream triangle for the tail. Squash it slightly and press lines down its length using the back of your knife. Stick it in place. Make four short cream fringed strips and stick one on each leg.

13 To make the flowers, thinly roll out about 60g (2oz) pink icing. Using the piping nozzle, cut out 5 discs per flower and arrange in circles on the board or unicorn's back (fig 2). Make a small flattened yellow ball for each centre.

fig 2

14 For the bow, thinly roll out 60g (2oz) pink icing. Cut two 5cm (2in) thin strips for the tails of the bow. Cut a "V" in one end of each strip and stick in place. Cut out another strip about 20cm (8in) long and bring the two ends towards the centre to make the loops. Stick on top of the pink tails. Cut a shorter 4cm (1 1/2in) strip and lay across the centre of the bow to neaten the middle.

TIP: If you don't want to sugarpaste the board, leave it plain or spread some green coloured buttercream "grass" around the covered cake instead.

Templates

All templates shown are actual size. Trace and then cut out.

Leaf

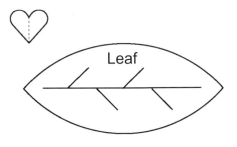

Dragon Eye

Car and Tractor Mudguard

Fairy wing

Leaf

Making a Piping Bag

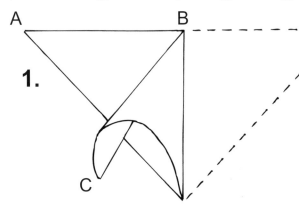

A   B   C

1.

C

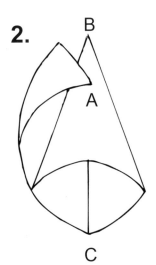

2.

B

A

C

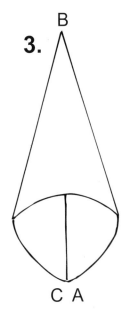

3.

B

C A

1 Make a greaseproof paper triangle and lay flat with the point towards you. Fold "C" over to form a cone.

2 Wrap "A" around the cone. "A" and "C" should be at the back and the tip should be sharp and pointed.

3 Fold "A" and "C" over a couple of times to hold the bag together. Place a little buttercream inside. Fold the top of the bag to close and snip a tiny triangle off the point.